Running Again
in Hollywood Cemetery

University of Central Florida Contemporary Poetry Series

Running Again
in Hollywood Cemetery

Poems by

Ron Smith

University of Central Florida Press
Orlando

This book
is dedicated to Delores

Contents

V

VI

VII

Acknowledgments

I am grateful to the editors of the following magazines in which these poems first appeared:

Arete: "Photograph of Jesse Owens at the Gun"
The Bennington Review: "At the Vietnam Memorial, 1983"
Bitterroot: "Wood"
College English: "Off the Corridor Near My Dying Grandfather"
The Crescent Review: "That Striped Cat," "Water Tower," "There"
Crosscurrents: "March"
The Georgia Review: "Declaiming," under the title "When My Father"
Kansas Quarterly: "Striking Out My Son in the Father-Son Game," "Knock"
The Kenyon Review: "Morning: Two Dogs on a Winter Field," "Oxford, 1975"
The Nation: "Bagging Leaves in March," "Leaving Forever"
New Virginia Review: "Iron," "Photograph of My Father and My Mother, 1946"
Poetry East: "War Stories"
Poetry Northwest: "For Mother, Who Thought Cremation Evil," "Railroad Track," "Sister"
The Richmond Quarterly: "Garden," "G.B., Skinning," "Waiting for You to Return from West Virginia," "Newspaper Photo of Hoffa Doing Pushups"
Southern Humanities Review: "Katie on Her Education"
Southern Poetry Review: "Running Again in Hollywood Cemetery"
University of Portland Review: "Fires," "Magnifying Glass"
The William and Mary Review: "Gatlinburg"
Wisconsin Review: "Errand"
Zone 3: "Queen's College, Oxford"

A special thanks to Dave Smith for his advice and encouragement.

I

At the Vietnam Memorial, 1983

"Clear the air! clean the sky! wash the wind!
    take the stone from the stone, take the skin
    from the arm, take the muscle from the
    bone, and wash them."

— *Murder in the Cathedral*

I fought
the March wind,
at each hill saying,
This is it. This looks new.
When I thought I had gone too far,

I was there. It's black, but
I had seen the pictures. I walked
beside a wall of small names
to find Wells and Strobo,
who never knew each other.

But they both loved fast cars
and hated school more than I did.
Which is why they are carved
in black and I can drive to see them.
I was in the back seat

when Wells slammed over a gas pump
and then filled up anyway.
And in the All-Star Game
tiny Strobo stole the headlines
from the big-name backs, zipped past

giants for the only touchdown.
He was too light
for a scholarship. He'd give
a kind of buck-toothed shrug and say,
I got a girl and a GTO.

Walking back to my Olds,
I sized up the Washington Monument,
measuring space
for a continent of names.
On every side of the Mall

the pale facades
rose like clouds.
Every marble column there,
every granite block waits
to spring back ten billion years

to a blinding stellar
vapor. Stone from stone,
hell. Every atom
shall be set
free.

II

Railroad Track

I sling my shoes to the edge of the yard
behind the house my father sold
to people I've never met
and go to feel the roughness of splintered ties
through the bare, thin soles of the present.
Between these rails, behind this house,
I am always an only child,
following this old spur
where a daydream nearly killed me once.

On this short line to the pulpwood plant
flatbeds rolled, throbbed our door frames
twice a day, chasing a horn
everybody said could raise the dead.
I bent for the blackberries' tiny grenades,
Hollywood bombs singing in my skull.
A man in a ratty garden was pointing,
his mouth open round
words that would not travel—

                              and the silence
went inside out, shook my chest with something
there all along and I turned to a
locomotive front like the wall of an iron cathedral,
a gargoyle engineer hanging from the sky, his face
twisting soundless curses, and a breath
before my legs melted I stepped
beyond the rails and the train,
the pitch of its howl dropping,
passed.

        In the quaking rocks close
to the shine of steel where wheel meets rail
like a razor on a metal strop,
I knelt until the pines came back
to the other side of the track and I could hear
mocking birds squabbling in the bushes
and the shrieks of girls far away
skipping rope safely in the street.

"You all right?" the old man called
from a row of stunted corn.
The rail joints clicked and clicked.
"Sure," I said. And I rose
on the same skinny legs
from the sting of river rocks
and tightroped the smooth silver home,
bowing that night before a steaming plate
in the soft chant of Mother's usual blessing,
hearing none of the words
and all of the tired low promise of protection.

Sister

Because she knew he wasn't under the sheet,
he would have to take her with him.
Under the sheet his head was his new glove
black in the moonlight, soft and fragrant
with saddle soap and stuffed with underwear,
and all the rest of him was a sleeping bag
curved and bunched like a shoulder, a hip,
crooked up like a pitcher's leg, just the way
he slept, like half way through his windup
before the leg came down and the ball
was there, already too close to hit or duck.

But he wouldn't take her with him,
and he lifted her off the cold grass
and pushed her back in the window,
both strong hands on her skinny butt.
Before he climbed over the red lights
and into the bed of the truck with all
the others and his arm around that one,
he promised her fifty baseball cards
complete with the crumbly pink gum
he always gave her anyway. Back before
the milkman, he said. Keep the window open.

She made him stand below her for awhile.
His eyes were big and he talked quiet
and fast the way he did before a game.
He told her to go back to her room.
He told her to dream of his fastball
to make it faster before Saturday,
and she tried to. She pushed in beside

the self he had left her. On the milky ceiling
the back yard where she caught his slow,
humpbacked pitches that still stung
like an ice pick through her hand changed

and drifted in a bright cloud of red dust
where his eyes under his cap narrowed
and went through her because her fingers
between her knees had to tell him what to throw
and she was smothered stiff and burning
under the chest protector and shin guards,
and his eyes wouldn't wait forever, narrowed more
between the bars on her face, the bat was too close
to her head, too close, and she wasn't ready,
but he nodded and started and the leg was up,
and she wasn't ready, she wasn't ready.

Iron

At Howard's Gym on Victory Drive
Royce and I gave our bodies to metal.
After a day burning in ditches
for five quarters an hour, we paid
Howard to arm us in his stinking hole
with iron flesh the scouts from Bama would buy.
We writhed on the dip bar to rise,

pumping for Howard's snake-sized veins,
frowned before the bullhorns of the tricep grip
to move a greasy cable an inch from our dripping noses,
strapped our skulls to black plates
that clanked between our knees, bowing and bowing
to a future where our heads were stuck on posts
of neck wider than our helmets.

We learned to cross our legs casually for form,
proud not to mention that the bench press bar was
     bending.
Through the steaming summer nights we wore
our fiercest masks of meat, grunting our reps,
making our sets. One more, you can do it, one more,
until the lean limbs of boyhood were gone
into the armor of the lineman's bulk.

We would circle Joe's at the end of August,
festoon car doors with our football beef,
circle all the others who had spent July
parked there with corndogs and cherry Cokes,
their arms dwindling around the waists of girls.
When one climbed out to slap our shoulders,
we flexed hard under every touch.

For Mother, Who Thought Cremation Evil

Blood flared in her brain
and she was speechless forever.
She watched the fire six cold months,
then I rolled her away from the hearth
to the sea and she watched that gray flame.
Life began in the sea, I hissed at her, close
enough to kiss, hoping to note the black
pupils zero down, the lips purse
for Genesis. Nothing. July,
even the watching was gone.

I gave her back the blurred face
of the man who early escaped her tongue.
I spoke of the Chrysler I climbed out of
under blackwalls still spinning, tangling
Spanish moss, of the mile she walked every morning
to stand behind the pies on the Woolworth's counter,
the rubbers I left drooling in her cool
starched sheets after each girl was gone,
how she damned me day and night, how
I never apologized for anything
and never wanted to.

Wind lifted the thin smoke
of her hair, showed the veiny shells
of her ears. Her body in my arms: light
as a bundle of driftwood. At the foot of the droning
Atlantic I laid us side by side, her in shade and

myself in sun, next to her gleaming wheel.
Her ashen profile, its lips parted
slightly as if to whisper,
faded

in the umbrella's dark,
and that preacher I see now
was a lover comes back to walk among
flaming azaleas in the big park after church.
They stand, both flushed and young, in the dapple
of water oaks, murmuring what only a child could
    believe
were the stone words of a god. I stomp through
pigeons old men lean slowly to feed. I scream
around and around the dazzling
fountain. She watches
his lips.

We would put her in the ground
and cover her up with Black Creek dirt,
just the way she wanted it. All that last month
the sea burned to deliver its boring sermon:
there is no hell, nothing will come of nothing,
your flesh crawls with the heat of a star
exploding, exploding, but not forever,
the bright blood of your eyelids
is the one true sky.

Water Tower

The wind behind us pulled on our packs.
Hands firmly on each steel rod, we were careful
to show we were never careful, even when
the ladder left the huge bolted leg to lean
for the catwalk circling above us like Saturn's rings.
A hundred feet above the streetlight
we unloaded blankets, bananas, and rum crooks.

Clenching our teeth on sweet tobacco,
we thought we had left town already.
Our dark neighborhoods at our feet,
the black sky strewn with close blue stars,
we matched nickels on the very top
and pulsed wholly red with warning
to pilots they were still too near the earth.

Our parents thought we hugged the ground
in the gnat-buzzing woods.
But even mosquitoes couldn't reach us up there.
Police Chief Crowder moved below us
in his slow square car, prowling the streets' angles,
throwing his yellow beam into the usual darkness,
behind the Webbers' cinder block garage, under
the Methodist preacher's hedges.

We slept on the catwalk along the curve of steel,
and seven of us, toe to head,
could surround the whole town's water.
We rose full of water in the dawn, shivering,
hanging long pisses to the familiar street,

trembling stiffly, quickly down the cold rungs,
while dogs harangued the milkman,
and the big trucks over on 17
made their hollow sounds passing through.

—for Stan

Photograph of My Father and My Mother, 1946

When I look at this, I become a street photographer
sprung like a thug before these tall,
handsome people. Above the loosened tie,
the clean jaw, the thin mustache,
his eyes drill me. He strides
in an easy march, sharp pleated,
a sweater vest tight to show muscles,
white sleeves rolled above tanned forearms
that hang a little out as if the punch
already moves down that straight spine
to the cupped hands that can wait
for the next stride.

And she too keeps coming, eyes close on me,
one shiny pump blurred below the perfect calf,
purse strap tight around her wrist.
Four buttons glint along the curve
from the tiny, belted waist to the flare
of collar at the smooth, white neck.
Her mouth hints at a smile.
I cannot tell they have just met.
His dark hand obscures her pale one,
but I cannot tell if they touch,
if he will have to release her to swing.

Of course, he will not swing. The war is over,
they have found each other, and they are so young.
I will step aside and smile and name my price,
and she will want the snapshot
neither expected nor asked for.
But first, his eyes lock hard on the camera,
a clear warning and a dare. She hangs back
a step, a coy tilt to her head, proud
of her beauty and her new suit and of
the man beside her who will protect her today
from the likes of me.

G.B., Skinning

Long black foot lashed
to the clothesline, dull knife
circling near the limit
of pulled-down skin where pale tissues
part like mist, black slick strip shines,
hangs from a hole on one side
of the hidden face, is a lip, he pulls
with both purple hands, sharp
points tightly clenched, back teeth
grin, grin, white, Lion's
Club ring clotted with matter, the eye,
the dark eye yields, bends
against the knife edge, will
not flinch, slit eyeball less
to him now than weight
of this sunlight

         cold spray
of black blood when the hide
strips off re-creates us: *Gross!*
Brian says and spits, I wipe
bare thighs with palms, palms
on T-shirt

       unzips
the belly to the breastbone,
guts the color of goat milk
lean, a sharp smell, saws
at a snake of guts, squeezes
two inches of green shit, *Shit!*
onto thick fingers already slinging

at the A&P bag beside his boots,
waves the hand in the plastic bucket's
cloudy water, trims all the insides
loose, pulls with the free hand
two lobes of light brown liver,
musk, yellow stomach no bigger
than an eye, lower and lower
it all hangs and glistens,
hacked, dumped in the bag.

G.B. opens the coon's chest
and squints inside like the TV sheriff
looking for a derringer. Sunlight
glows through backflesh, and white
ribs curve in a perfect order.
Gone leave them kidneys, G.B. says,

lives on past that seventy to ninety,
tells hunting stories when we visit,
squeezing our shoulder muscles
till we yell, slapping our broadening backs,
saying, *Damn, you're a biggun. You
getting any out there at that college?*
and winks.

Off the Corridor,
Near My Dying Grandfather

As I go by, I see a man
cramming his face
into a cup, gripping the smudged styrofoam
with two bruised hands,
bony elbows on bony knees,
his head in a cloud of steam.
Tall beside him stands Mother,
tightlipped, two more
volcanic coffees in her fists.

She's been sobering up
brothers all her life.
The flesh on her face
retreats toward the sockets,
toward eyes that see
the same face
in all these family faces.

I never break stride
toward the door
marked exit and will not
turn my head again
to the cloudy mirrors
behind the lilies
in the lobby.

Newspaper Photo
of Hoffa Doing Pushups

Of course, the bloated
fat-cat leers of pleasure,
faces ugly and anonymous
as beer bellies.
Some witty photographer
has trapped two buddies
in the upper corners
where the lens melts them
toward what we think
they are.

But Hoffa is down,
thick fingers on the floor,
in his tuxedo, looking up
at us here in the future
where we know nothing
about him now. Some dame
in old movie diamonds
squints like a severe
mother at the square-headed
man with the boy's eyes
that hold us, that say,
Look at me. Look.
I'm so young
and strong tonight.

There

The gold gleam hurts from the water, flickers
with blackness of walking figures, hurts again
deep into the eye, sun or reflection of sun,
and black shapes move in it, right to left.
I am in bed and not yet dreaming. I open
my eyes and there is only paleness, only
finer and finer shades of gray the blinds
make on the ceiling. Eyes close,
the gold gleam hurts.
They must be men, they walk
with sticks, and this is a child, and this
one has breasts and carries something
on its back. They look down at the beach,
if it is a beach, they are thin, there is no sound.
They are not going home.

III

Leaving Forever

My son can look me level in the eyes now,
and does, hard, when I tell him he cannot watch
chainsaw murders at the midnight movie,
that he must bend his mind to Biology,
under this roof, in the clear light of a Tensor lamp.
Outside, his friends throb with horsepower
under the moon.

         He stands close, milk sour
on his breath, gauging the heat of my conviction,
eye-whites pink from his new contacts.
He can see me better than before. And I can see
myself in those insolent eyes, mostly head
in the pupil's curve, closed in by the contours
of his unwrinkled flesh.

         At the window he waves
a thin arm and his buddies squall away in a glare
of tail lights. I reach out my hand to his shoulder,
but he shrugs free and shows me my father's narrow
    eyes,
the trembling hand at my throat, the hard wall
at the back of my skull, the raised fist framed
in the bedroom window I had climbed through
at 3 A.M.

       "If you hit me, I'll leave forever,"
I said. But everything was fine in a few days, fine.

"I would have come back," I said, "false teeth and all."
Now, twice a year after the long drive, in the yellow light
of the front porch, I breathe in my father's whiskey,
ask for a shot, and see myself distorted in
his thick glasses, the two of us grinning,
as he holds me with both hands at arm's length.

IV

Katie on Her Education

I went down to the river to walk
and to hear all those tons of water
the earth lured down from Virginia hills
as you lured me, and in the middle of the clay
path I met the man who'd taught
me how to think after you had
taught me how to feel.

He was with a woman not his kindly
coffee-bringing wife. And his face was raw
with guilt. And his eyes were jerky with lies.
"Hello, Katie," he said in a gathering bass.
"We were trying to decide what kind of birds
those are," he said, Dr. Warner, who taught me
Ethics, who demanded such care with words,

said. In the huge, white-dead tree
were huge, black-still birds.
"Crows, I believe," I said.
Everybody knows crows. Her face was white
as the tree and the water-rounded rocks.
We smiled a stiff set of smiles.
And then he led

her away. One day when we
have not fought I'll take you there
to walk the river's run,
to let you know I
know just where
the crows along the river
roost and why.

War Stories

What makes her climb him
with a voice like spikes
when he bangs the screen door
after work? He hangs
in the air all week,
sweating over missed connections,
canceling time zones
with copper wire, making
a Northwest Passage in the sky.
He burns against creosote poles
the colors of girls

of the Solomons where he moved
through bullet-shredded jungles
because he was seventeen
and sick of the long hot rows of tobacco.
Or pretends he's a sniper
strapped forever in the top
of a palm, drills
passing drivers with his stare
until dead in the silent hover
that could keep a squad belly down
in the mud all day.

Home, the slow tick
of a cheap wall clock
in a steaming house,
the slow tear or sweat
from her there eternally
at the iron or stove,
the hateful sideways

slant of the eyes
that says he betrayed—
what?

At the metal kitchen table
he drinks beer before supper
and thinks of that captain's eyes
when a private tripped
on a still warm sentry and fell
between the leg-sized roots
of a banyan. The captain crouched
inside the tree, a .45
trembling in his fist, wide eyes
blue as acetylene.

The fall, gentle and long in his head,
the captain aiming the huge barrel
at his face and firing
nothing but a loud click.
Then, Jesus, cocking the piece
and aiming again,
and a high voice now
in a jabber of English,
Captain, it's me, it's me—
scrambling forward
on his elbows to bury
his bayonet in the man
before the explosion.

War stories, war stories,
she says in the dark
after the poker game.
Her hair smells like smoke.
When are you going to grow up, she says.
Softball tournament Saturday, he says,
pulling at her hip bone,
trying to turn her toward him.
She holds her small belly

in both hands like a wound.
All the wives will be there, he says,
You'll love it. You always love it.

Waiting for You
to Return from West Virginia

With his perfect pitch, our son
has taught himself to play the guitar
his grandfather left behind.

The boy has tuned the woman-shape

like a mandolin. Foot on his knapsack,
he bends, head turned. Notes
hang near him in the firelight

like whispers. They vanish. They begin.

He can't change chords, doesn't know
he wants to. A book of poems
lies open, heavy on my lap.

Outside, the cold wind yearns in the treetops.

March

Her fingers are long and loose on the dark
handle. The leaves crackle and waft, and
she stretches to bring them to her.
March is wrong for raking, but she has found
a thousand oak leaves in the boxwoods,
dead leaves that leap and leap for her.

And at her back snowflakes mingle with forsythia,
and beyond that, beyond the greening honeysuckle
welded to the rusty fence, boys in red caps
squawk and spread their arms in the delicate
dance of waiting under high flies, eyes up
as if they, too, thought this sky were a miracle.

She leans on the rake and flips her bangs
with a puff of white breath. When she frowns
at her palms for blisters, I can feel her callus
snag on the flesh of my stomach. She
is there, drawing winter away from our house.
She thinks I am here, warm by the fire, writing
a poem about loneliness and the tight grip of death.

—for Delores

That Striped Cat

my wife brought back from the mountains
meant nothing to me. Another mouth
to feed. A luxurious-stretching, lithe,
temporary thing that rubbed itself
predictably against our legs
at dinner.

        But Sunday I found him standing
between the holly bush and the front stoop
on a fat squirrel. He raised
his changed eyes
to my voice and dropped
the dark wedge of head.

        Monday, another
bellydown squirrel, muscles bunched
motionless under the soft gray fur,
its winter thickened tail moving
on what little breeze could reach it
between the sharp holly and the concrete slab.
Over by the gutter, two yellow eyes
in the boxwoods, the brazen, helpless,
sated eyes of the love-enslaved.

        I haven't
belled him yet. After dinner
I take his warm weight
into my lap. My wife

won't touch him. Murderer,
she says, I want him gone.
I'll bell him, I say and push
the loose, furred flesh
back and forth across his bones.

Knock

There was a knock
at the back of his face.
He wouldn't open up.

Through the peephole
he could see only
that it was dark
and powerfully muscled.

That might have been rain
on its cheek.

"I'm all right,"
he told the woman
who showed him a pair
of concerned eyes.

He will not tell her
that his outside
has become his inside.
Now she is in.

They will have
to make do
with a long loneliness.

Gatlinburg

Beyond the cheese balls a man
the size of a lemon slice
is casting for trout.

His feet throb with the cold.
The Cabbage Patch woman drinks him
then goes back to the salad bar.

You have just told me to by God fuck off.
Everything on my plate is green
under the fluorescent lights.

You chew a line deeper
into the corners of your mouth.
The yellow slicker and black boots

move out of sight below us
then reappear to my right, downstream.
Cast and cast. The room is aquamarine.

The fisherman licks his tiny chapped lips
and looks right at you.

Morning: Two Dogs
on a Winter Field

Soundless,
breaths floating together
before the sun, black
labs tumbled slowly
in their own
corona,

beyond male and female, wheeling
over the frozen earth,
dark bodies
burning.

Queen's College, Oxford

As much to escape the rain
as to see sights, we crossed
the sole-hollowed threshold
of the chapel. Under Thornhill's
Ascension, she arched her back
in that gray sweater until my breath
was gone again.

                    I'll bet all
your ceilings are blank, she said
in those broad, foreign vowels
as if blankness were something
she would love to swallow,
and she pushed her face into my side.

Above us, thick-armed angels
carried Jesus away through a hole
in the clouds. In the cherub-
crowded air near his head,
his palms opened, left, right.
The sun shone through the rips.

He was losing his vestments
in the wind of their departure,
the blue cloak unfurling
from his hairless chest
like fabric of sky.

                    I wish
I could believe like that, I said.
See how their eyes roll up
with ecstasy? Ooooo, I know
that feeling, she said.

Oxford, 1975

If we had not gone there, away
from our real lives, gone
to drift along the Cherwell
in a haze of good sherry, recline
on elbows by the Isis
like people in ads,

we wouldn't have seen
those spires blacken against
the sky's vast burn and ribboning,
or leaned together
down the High in the hush
of dinner-time shadows, sleeping,

nearly, between our steps,
the day settling
like influenza along our bones,
or found ourselves at twilight
behind the flutist
in his tattered gown
drawing us into Longwall

with, yes, "Scarborough Fair,"
black gown floating away,
invisible roses trellised
on the faint smell of soot,
that simple melody
pulling itself out of our hearts

like guilt, like sweet confession,
until, at a turning, the rush
of traffic tore something

from the air, and he strolled,
just a student, flute
swinging at the end of his arm

like the spit hung silver in your snapshot
of a boy on Magdalen Bridge,
and we knew,
without speaking, without
leaning apart to see our eyes,
that we loved each other
and that it would never be enough.

V

Declaiming

When my father takes my poems
in his fight-broken hands,
he holds my few words
at arm's length,
raises his rich, unused voice,
and calls each syllable
so carefully you can see
him declaiming Bryant
fifty years ago, at attention
beside his lunch pail
in the single room of Stilson School.

There, his cheeks are full of blood,
and he is handsome.
Parris Island is two years north.
He smells like the cows he milked
in the early Georgia dark.
He moves down each row
of phrases with the grimness
of those who feel
they must make the earth yield
its sweet corn,
its crouching Japanese,
catching up against
hard roots, going on

up the burning islands of the Pacific,
peering into the flaring dark
of each step north.
Against beachhead sunsets he sees
the Zeros sputter and go down.

In foxhole after foxhole he dreams
of dusty fields where he falls
behind the mule
and the rows close over him
and he comes up changed,
atabrine yellow,
wavering in the merest breeze,
his body whispering.

The days have gathered
into straight lines behind him.
After half a century
of the silent heft of steel
he is left again with a handful
of someone else's words,
words that slip
between the thick, crooked fingers
like the lightest of seeds.

VI

Magnifying Glass

The tiny ant swells and swells and bursts
in a shrinking halo under the glass. Worse
things happen every day, we
could argue. I watch from the window, freed
by dark screens from a father's duty.
He has been studying science, ready
to explode some innards now
for the sake of discovering how
the clockwork works— or doesn't.
I'm not surprised that last month he wasn't
a killer of any sort, that he cried
when told his long-suffering turtle had died
a peaceful death. Last summer he screamed
to stop me from gassing the huge black ants streaming
from the white oak I had split. Today, his eyes
go narrow with concentration. They clench against the
    light,
then, with each new death, flare wide. Today, in rare
February sun he kneels in play and a kind of prayer.

—for Brooks

Striking Out My Son
in the Father-Son Game

Caught in the open in broad daylight,
jerky-eyed with doubt,
he swings like someone
who's never held a bat.

His elbows wrongly angle in,
his wrists are snapless
when the soft, lopsided sphere
drops from the sky.

Anyway, those wobbly ankles
and rattly knees cannot
spank those Nikes off the bases
or make a proper feet-first slide.

His eyes are everywhere
but on the ball. I arc
three adequate pitches
and retire the side.

We joke our stiff adult jokes
to the plate and cock
our clubs at our squawking,
crouching sons.

Despite the jolt to dozing muscles,
we find we can still hit
and run. Bellies leaning
toward the outfield,

we circle and circle the bags.
On the mound a grim boy tiptoes
to see his best pitch ride
into the left field pines.

Another banker scores.
My son slinks among a dozen fielders,
trying to hide.
He will have to come

to the plate again
with that gap between his fists
I haven't made him close.
I climb the red clay,

toe the rubber, and spit.
From a row of hooting women
my wife glares at me
through the shimmer of heat.

She can see the blood in my face
that means the steeper drop,
the slow backspin. These little boys
will never hit me today.

Bagging Leaves in March

Heft the clean folded bag, creamy to your fingers,
shiny in the sun. Snap it open and let the wind
fill it, stretching its creases out, tugging to work.
Scoop and scoop the brittle handfuls till the dustgrit
goes to slime and earthy smell. Dangle a pink worm
speckled with dirt crumbs and count its pullups,
its liquid oozy going, its wrinkled, fattening coming
    back.

The grass, you will find, is nearly white.
Pull your tragic faces, loving the chance to make it
green again, loving the black kordite
roughed plump with a load of lightness.
Love the final spin you give it, the stiff
yellow twist to keep death in its place.

Wood

My wood is split and stacked
in angular perfection.
The yard smells
like strange fruit.
Black ants came out
like guilt when
my ax broke those barrelshapes.

White oak and red oak
have broken my
skin with splinters.
And made me grunt
with lifting.
And rubbed my shoulderbones
to fresh, fresh strawberries.

Fires

This November fire drops perfect cubes of glowing
Oak and heats the house to a kind of womb.
So much for the shaggy threat that loomed
Over the roof for green decades. I know
Where its weight is now. It will not trouble
Me now with dreams of its knotted arms, doom
Heavy with growing, tearing through my rooms.
This wedge of oak broke brittle from double
Bladed ax which April made me swing
In lumberjack clothes and a Sunday stubble
Of graying beard. Fires for the coming snow.
Who thinks of the cold in the thawing spring?
Though I chopped, I thought of only two things:
How safe the roof, how solid each blow.

Errand

Eyes afire with seeing
its first headlights, the fawn
turns and leaps after its mother
who hung beside the moon
above the fence wire
and was gone. The fawn
cannot find a way, bucks
hard into the dark
honeysuckle again, again, falls
shivering back each time
the hidden steel stops him,
flexes at the edge of the ditch
an instant to leap again
too low. It's all right,
I say, It's all right, following
my long shadow to him. His hooves
churning blackberries, his head
straining through a rusted hole,
my hand hovering over his dappled
back, I bend and see what he sees:
the faint glint of her eyes
at the far edge of stony field.
And now her shape, motionless
as certainty. He wheels
from me, clatters across
the macadam, and a line
of birches takes him in, closes

a strip of night firmly
behind the tail's white flicker.

Why am I trembling? There's nothing
there but my old Omega,
throbbing out of time.
I walk back
into its cold wash of light.

Garden

A tractor snorts and clears its oily throat.
A fence has grown around this field of mud
Where not too long ago a garden stood.
This was a pleasant bower, as remote
Among man's structures as the evening note
Of the hidden dove. And now the thud
Of the tamper tamping, the thwack of stud
Stunned by the hammer. Like pollen, sawdust floats.

In one missed corner forsythia climbs
The air. A jonquil wears a smear of dirt.
Sentimental? Men made the garden. Who's hurt
By the loss of a few flowers, by the crud
Of construction? Are office buildings crimes?
We dig foundations. Men bend, harvesting mud.

Photograph of Jesse Owens
at the Gun

Beneath a puff of white gun smoke a man
the shade of cinders has risen
from between white lines
at an angle sharp with speed.
He is himself a thrust of angles:
one foot down, one hand reaching,
elbow, knee, the single bend at the waist,
all his flesh strung tight.

In the background row of pale blurred faces
these who appear to wear his colors
must be his teammates.
We can tell only that
they do not seem to cheer.
Behind them the tiers of Berlin
mass into gray clouds.

All the races of 1936 are stopped
inside this black frame.
The man whose captured body
pulls us to the wall
cannot reach the tape, his form
caught here in the rough shape
of the swastikas that fly in the corner.

Nothing moves, nothing changes.
We stare and stare.

—for DS, CK, and TH

VII

Running Again
in Hollywood Cemetery

December: Richmond, Virginia

Nothing's changed here
since you and I climbed the sagging
chain link and honeysuckle
off Cherry St. to sprint the steep hills
of the dead. We knew what we wanted:
granite thighs for trampling linemen,
legs that could launch us over the caged faces
to break the plane between us
and gold figures we envisioned marching
across our mantels; women whose red lips
glistened and parted for everything
we could give them.

Coach ordered hills
so we ran here in a pumping race to this crest
where we stomped two presidents
with our breakdown drills,
where this stained woman still bends
a face I will never see into her metal hands.
Neither falling behind, we took each other
on a tour of lies, past the white slab
where you laid Sandy and showed your ass
to a screaming widow who lashed you bloody
with a dozen roses while you by God
went on and finished,

past the filth-eyed angels
drooping with sorrow, shrouded obelisks

and artfully broken columns,
sandstone tree trunks carved intricate
with rot, the gothic Randolph tomb
where I crowbarred the bronze
one August afternoon on Laura's dare,
where the west window broke the darkness
into colors over her shivers, and she laid back,
the Virgin's blue cloak across her scar
and my chest war painted,

and she said, I'm safe,
and I didn't believe her and spilled my seed
in Randolph's deep-carved name.
Which were the lies? Was the heavy door
already open? Did I really pour myself
into that gray stone? In the locker room your skinny ass
never had a scratch that I remember.
And what do we have now? Your Saturday
headlines have shrunk to one small name
in black marble not far from Lincoln's huge,
tired eyes in that other capital we cursed
with our simple history.

Alone in Vermont ice
I've tried to chase it all down,
pound some sense into it, like the time
I bloodied knuckles on Jeff Davis's cold jaw
and then on you because you thought
my whiskey meanness was Yankee sacrilege.
In the blinding light at breakfast we blamed
our bloody shirts and fist-changed faces
on the Church Hill boys.

Since then I've run
more miles than you ever ventured from home,
even for that jungle assault when
you came up vapor just before
your first R&R. They went back and back

for a week after pushing past that blasted clearing.
Nothing, not a dog tag, not a silver filling.
In the only letter you ever finished
you wrote of another city you never laid eyes on,
dreamed of yellow-faced women waiting
to set you on fire with
American diseases.

Today, lean for distance,
I have circled all the unchanging dead
with only a little chest burn, chasing
my breath up and down every hill I could find.
The pencil-necked guard who scared us away
in '65 is white-headed now, and almost fat.
He still chains the gate at sundown.
As early gold takes the Confederate pyramid
and every plinth and angel, a couple, arm and arm,
is walking on the flaming river far below.
I turn back for the granite arch
while there is still time.

Author's photo by Brooks R. Smith

About the Author

Born in Savannah, Georgia, Ron Smith now lives in Richmond, Virginia, where he is chairman of the Department of English at St. Christopher's School. He has taught creative writing at the University of Richmond and Virginia Commonwealth University, institutions from which he holds an M.A. in English and an M.F.A. in creative writing, and has lectured in modern American poetry at Mary Washington College.

Ron Smith has won a number of awards for his poetry, including the 1986 Guy Owen Prize from the *Southern Poetry Review*. He has been a Roper Graduate Fellow in English and a Bread Loaf Scholar in Poetry. *Running Again in Hollywood Cemetery* is his first book.

Library of Congress Cataloging in Publication Data

Smith, James Ronald
  Running again in Hollywood cemetery : poems / by Ron Smith
      p. cm. — (University of Central Florida contemporary
  poetry series)
    ISBN 0-8130-0881-6 (alk. paper)
    I. Title.   II. Series.
  PS3569.M537963R8   1988
  813′.54— dc19   88-2628
                                                            CIP

University Presses of Florida is the central agency for scholarly
publishing of the State of Florida's university system, pro-
ducing books selected for publication by the faculty editorial
committees of Florida's nine public universities: Florida A&M
University (Tallahassee), Florida Atlantic University (Boca
Raton), Florida International University (Miami), Florida State
University (Tallahassee), University of Central Florida (Or-
lando), University of Florida (Gainesville), University of North
Florida (Jacksonville), University of South Florida (Tampa),
University of West Florida (Pensacola).
  Orders for books published by all member presses should be
addressed to University Presses of Florida, 15 NW 15th Street,
Gainesville, FL 32603.